Millie Marotta's

Island Escape

T0347704

First published in the United Kingdom in 2022 by B.T. Batsford Ltd
43 Great Ormond Street
London WC1N 3HZ
An imprint of B.T. Batsford Holdings Ltd

ISBN: 9781849947756

A CIP catalogue record for this book is available from the British Library.

30 29 28 27 26 25 24 23 22
10 9 8 7 6 5 4 3 2 1

Reproduction by Mission Productions, Hong Kong
Printed by Vivar Printing Sdn. Bhd., Malaysia

FSC
www.fsc.org
MIX
Paper from
responsible sources
FSC® C084469

Millie Marotta's

Island
Escape

a colouring adventure

BATSFORD

Introduction

Islands are extraordinary places, home to a magnificent array of plants and animals often found nowhere else on Earth. Hosting every habitat imaginable – rainforests, mountains, volcanoes and swamps – islands come in all shapes and sizes and are found in every corner of the globe. Some stand alone and isolated thousands of miles offshore, battered by harsh elements, while others make up vast archipelagos, verdant and teeming with life.

Islands can be magical, often conjuring thoughts of adventure, mystery and wonder. You will find them aplenty in *Island Escape*, from tiny Skomer Island right here on my doorstep in Pembrokeshire, Wales, to the world's oldest island, Madagascar. This book celebrates the remarkable species found only on islands. These castaways, cut-off from their mainland cousins, have over time developed habits and ways to survive and thrive – often becoming distinct species altogether, unique in both appearance and behaviour. Over thousands of years, some grew smaller, such as the pygmy racoon of Cozumel Island in Mexico. Others lost specific abilities, such as the takahe of South Island, New Zealand, who, with no ground predators, lost the ability to fly.

But while many island species have made remarkable adaptations in order to survive, they are especially vulnerable to changes in their surroundings. If their habitat is damaged or destroyed, or their food source disappears, there is nowhere else for them to go. And all too many are already at increasing risk from rising sea levels, climate change and other environmental factors.

Island Escape champions just a few of the unique species that make islands their home, including the peculiar hump-nosed lizard, the elegant red-tailed tropicbird, the charismatic Bornean orangutan and the adorable pygmy three-toed sloth – a laid-back Caribbean islander who takes life at its own pace.

Relax and unwind as you island-hop your way around the globe and immerse yourself in an island paradise where lizards lounge and sea birds soar. Marvel at the formidable Komodo dragon and revel at the beauty of the Mariana fruit dove.

Whatever tickles your colouring taste buds, enjoy escaping to your very own island wonderland, bringing its inhabitants alive with colour. Shade in the shimmering inky plumage of the ribbon-tailed astrapia and the soft shades of mountain orchids, the iridescent hues of the red-tailed golden arowana and the kaleidoscopic colours of the Socotran chameleon.

As I often say in my introductions – because it's so true – I love making these books. They are, in fact, a rather selfish pursuit, allowing me to spend my days indulging in my two loves: art and nature. And I am inspired by how many of you enjoy my books for discovering more about the natural world as well as for your love of colouring and being creative. Making these books means that I am constantly learning myself and I'm thrilled to be able to share that with you. So, for the enquiring minds among you eager to learn about the species you are colouring, there is a glossary at the back of the book.

You'll also find lots of opportunity to add your own touches to the drawings themselves and I encourage you to do so, be it by creating entire backgrounds or adding tiny embellishments; I love seeing how the illustrations in my books evolve into unique artworks as each of you inject your own creative vision. You'll also find tester pages at the back for trying out your materials and colour palettes.

As the world remains a challenging place at times, I know colouring and creative activities play a role in helping us take care of our mental wellbeing, and the same can be said for spending time in nature. And there is no better combination, as far as I am concerned, than art and nature. So, whether you colour to get your creative fix or for a spot of much-needed mindfulness, with *Island Escape* I welcome you to the wonders of our natural world and the joy of bringing each species alive with colour.

Your island-hopping adventure awaits!

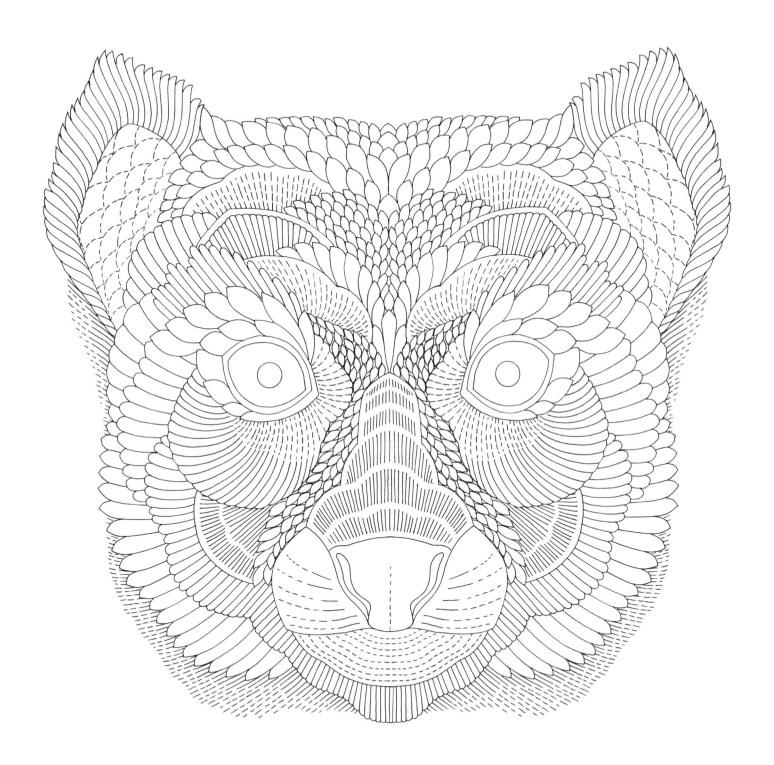

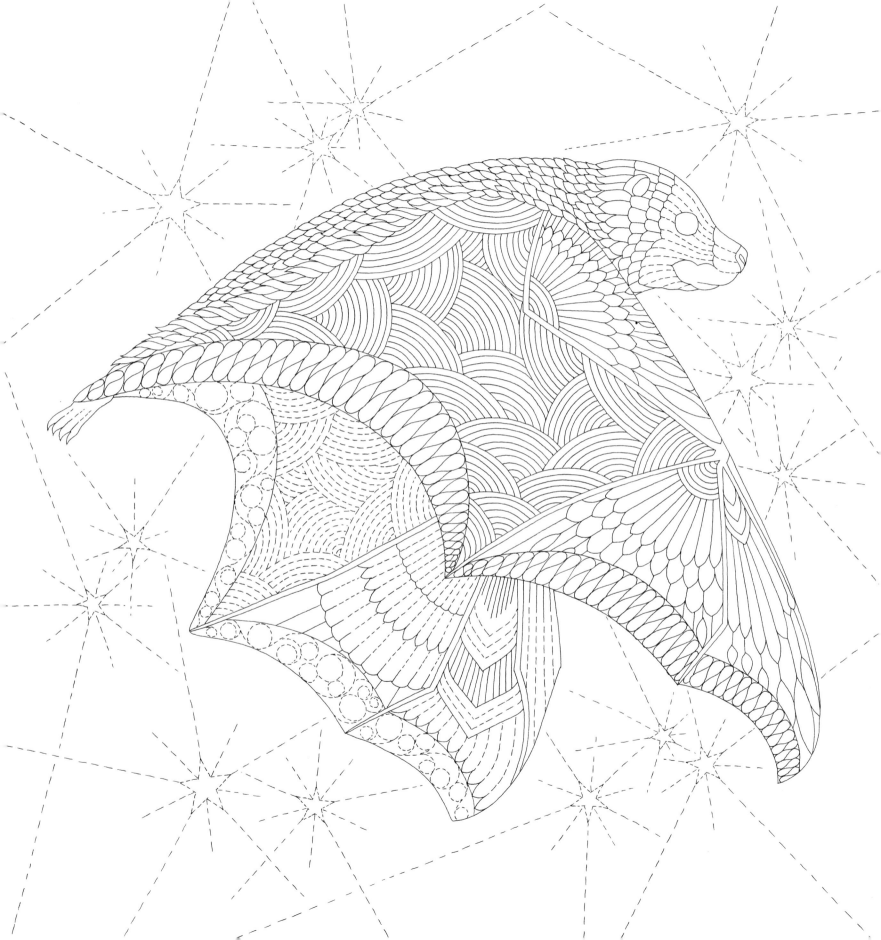

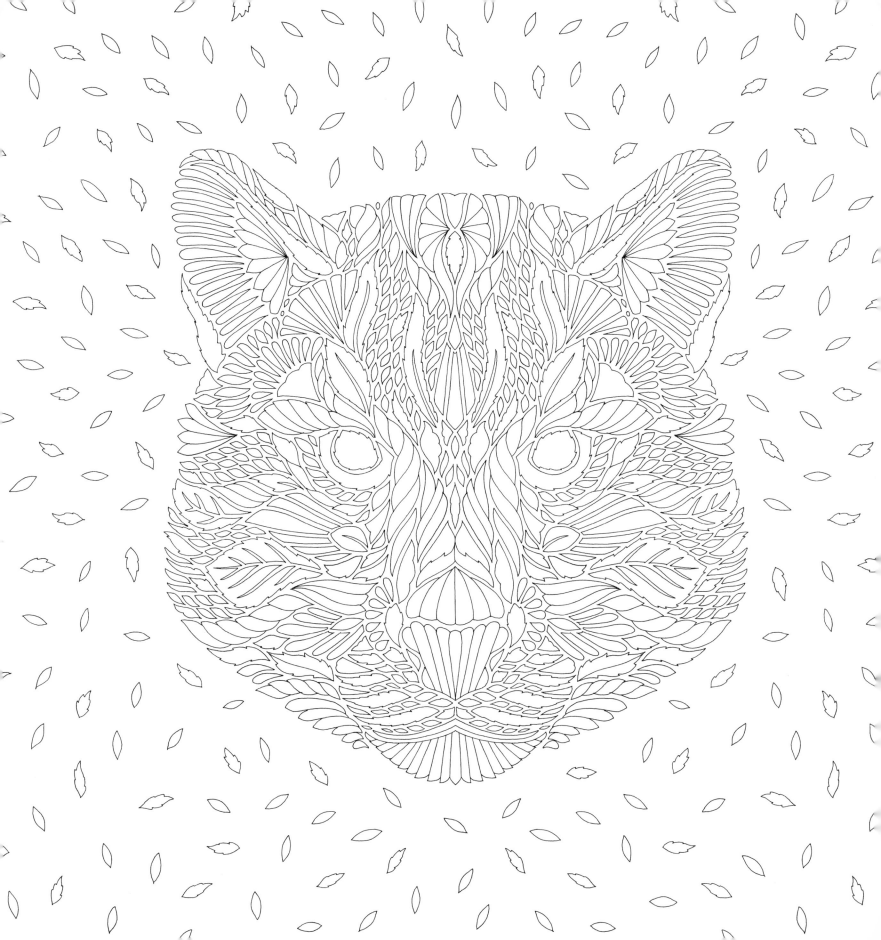

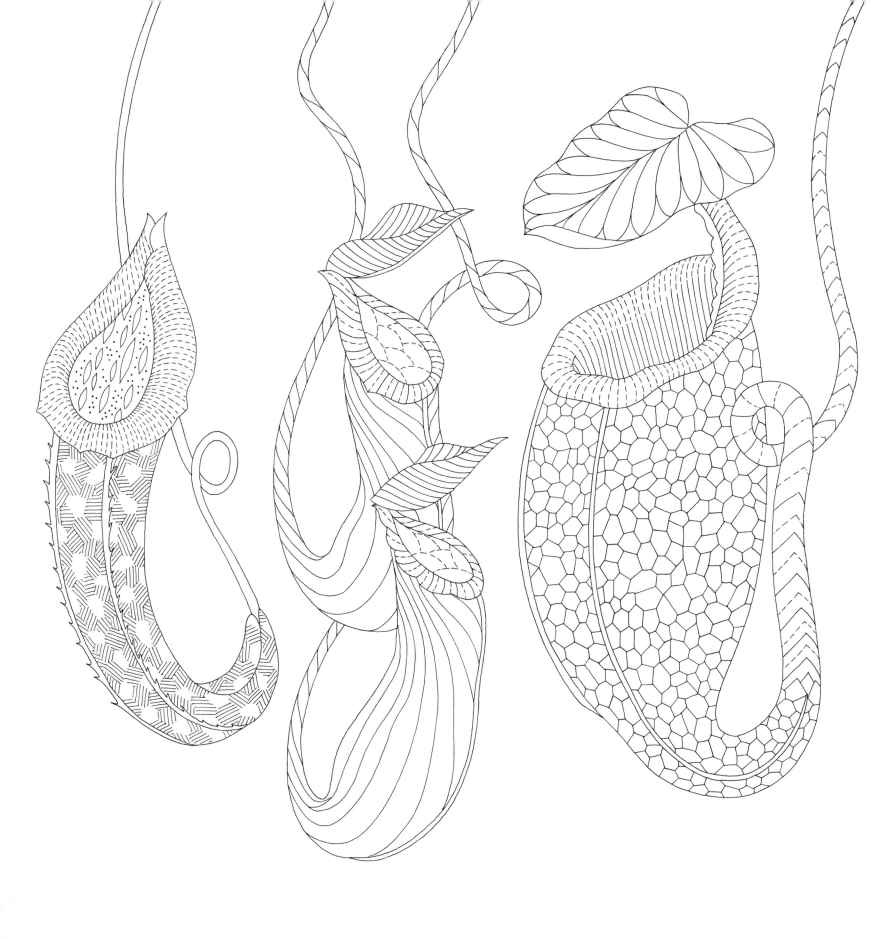

List of Creatures in *Island Escape*

Borneo pygmy elephant
(*Elephas maximus borneensis*)

Greater bamboo lemur
(*Prolemur simus*)

Angonoka or ploughshare
tortoise (*Astrochelys yniphora*)

Ribbon-tailed astrapia
(*Astrapia mayeri*)

Pygmy three-toed sloth
(*Bradypus pygmaeus*)

Laysan duck (*Anas laysanensis*)

Red-tailed tropicbird
(*Phaethon rubricauda*)

Bare-legged owl
(*Margarobyas lawrencii*)

Hump-nosed lizard
(*Lyriocephalus scutatus*)

Pittas
Azure-breasted pitta
(*Pitta steerii*)
Black-faced pitta (*Pitta anerythra*)
Superb pitta (*Pitta superba*)
Whiskered pitta (*Erythropitta kochi*)

Formosan rock macaque
(*Macaca cyclopis*)

Mauritian flying fox (*Pteropus niger*)

Tsushima Island marten
(*Martes melampus tsuensis*)

South Island takahe
(*Porphyrio hochstetteri*)

Forktail blue-eye or forktail
rainbowfish (*Pseudomugil furcatus*)

Tufted pygmy squirrel
(*Exilisciurus whiteheadi*)

Bornean orangutan
(*Pongo pygmaeus*)

Socotran chameleon
(*Chamaeleo monachus*)

Hawaiian monk seal
(*Neomonachus schauinslandi*)

São Tomé giant reed frog
(*Hyperolius thomensis*)

Island darter (*Sympetrum nigrifemur*)

Island fox (*Urocyon littoralis*)

Dragon blood tree (*Dracaena
cinnabari*) and Socotran white-eye
(*Zosterops socotranus*)

Hawaiian honeycreepers
'I'iwi or scarlet Hawaiian
honeycreeper (*Drepanis coccinea*)
'Apapane Hawaiian
honeycreeper (*Himatione
sanguinea*)
Kaua'i 'amakihi Hawaiian
honeycreeper (*Chlorodrepanis
stejnegeri*)

New Caledonian crested gecko
(*Correlophus ciliatus*)

Painted ringtail possum
(*Pseudochirulus forbesi*)

Comet moth (*Argema mittrei*)

Fossa (*Cryptoprocta ferox*)

Yellow-bellied sunbird-asity
(*Neodrepanis hypoxantha*)

Vancouver Island marmot
(*Marmota vancouverensis*)

Sri Lankan junglefowl
(*Gallus lafayettii*)

Sri Lankan pit viper
(*Trimeresurus trigonocephalus*)

Iriomote wild cat
(*Prionailurus bengalensis iriomotensis*)

Floreana mockingbird (*Mimus
trifasciatus*) and Galápagos prickly
pear (*Opuntia galapageia*)

Scilly bee (*Bombus muscorum
var. scyllonius*)

Cozumel or pygmy raccoon
(*Procyon pygmaeus*)

Maltese ruby tiger moth
(*Phragmatobia fuliginosa
ssp. Melitensis*)

Red-tail golden arowana
(*Scleropages aureus*)

Beautiful goetzea
(*Goetzea elegans*)

Narcondam hornbill
(*Rhyticeros narcondami*)

Philippine mouse-deer or balabac
chevrotain (*Tragulus nigricans*)

Verreaux's sifaka
  (*Propithecus verreauxi*)
Tamaraw or Mindoro dwarf
  buffalo (*Bubalus mindorensis*)
Tagimoucia (*Medinilla waterhousei*)
Lundy cabbage flea beetle
  (*Psylliodes luridipennis*)
Jellyfish tree (*Medusagyne oppositifolia*)
Bronze quoll (*Dasyurus spartacus*)
Japanese hare (*Lepus brachyurus*)
Orchids
  Pseudovanilla foliata
  Dryadorchis dasystele
  Diplocaulobium regale
  Bulbophyllum pseudotrias
  Bulbophyllum geniculiferum
  Bulbophyllum artostigma
Skomer vole (*Myodes
  glareolus skomerensis*)
Ray-finned fish
  (*Sinogastromyzon puliensis*)
Jamaican tody (*Todus todus*)
Javan Rhinoceros
  (*Rhinoceros sondaicus*)
Solomon Islands skink
  (*Corucia zebrata*)
Manus green tree snail
  (*Papustyla pulcherrima*)
Svalbard reindeer
  (*Rangifer tarandus platyrhynchus*)

Antillean palm swift
  (*Tachornis phoenicobia*)
Queen Alexandra's birdwing
  (*Ornithoptera alexandrae*)
Cape Verde spiny lobster
  (*Palinurus charlestoni*)
Maltese flowers
  Maltese sand crocus
    (*Romulea variicolor*)
  Maltese sea chamomile
    (*Anthemis urvilleana*)
  Maltese rock centaury
    (*Cheirolophus crassifolius*)
  Zerapha's sea lavender
    (*Limonium zeraphae*)
Abbott's booby (*Papasula abbotti*)
Andaman cobra (*Naja sagittifera*)
Pitcher plants
  Nepenthes veitchii
  Nepenthes alata
  Nepenthes bicalcarata
  Nepenthes stenophylla
  Nepenthes rajah
  Nepenthes lowii
Japanese serow
  (*Capricornis crispus*)
Mariana fruit dove
  (*Ptilinopus roseicapilla*)
Ascension Island crab
  (*Johngarthia lagostoma*)

Galápagos miconia
  (*Miconia robinsoniana*)
Komodo dragon
  (*Varanus komodoensis*)
Carola's parotia (*Parotia carolae*)

Test your colour palettes and materials here...

Also from Millie Marotta